A Glass Jar

Sarah Ridley

FRANKLIN WATTS
LONDON · SYDNEY

First published in 2006 by
Franklin Watts
338 Euston Road
London NW1 3BH

Franklin Watts Australia
Hachette Children's Books
Level 17/207 Kent Street
Sydney NSW 2000

ISBN: 0 7496 6058 9
Dewey number: 666'.1

Series editor: Sarah Peutrill
Art director: Jonathan Hair
Design: Jemima Lumley

Photo credits: James L. Amos/Corbis: 22, 27bl. Ancient Art & Architecture
Collection/Topfoto: 9b. Arco/La Terra Magica/Alamy: 16b, 26cr. Yann Arthus-
Bertrand/Corbis: 7t. Justin Case/Alamy: 30bl. Corbis: 25b. Bob Daemmrich/Image
Works/Topfoto: 5t. Digital Vision: front cover cl, 6b, 11t, 15b, 26cl. DK Limited/Corbis: 8t,
26tl. Mary Evans Picture Library: 19b. Mark E. Gibson/Corbis: 10t. Jeff Greenberg/Image
Works/Topfoto: 13b. Reino Hanninen/Alamy: 6t. Holt Confer/Image Works/Topfoto:
15c. Andre Jenny/Alamy: 31b. Sandi McDonald/Alamy: 31lt. Ray Moller/Watts: front
cover tl & b, back cover tl, 1, 4, 5b, 23br, 27br. Kevin R. Morris/Bohemian Nomad
Picturemakers/Corbis: 10b. Pilkington plc: front cover tc, 17bl, 17br, 26tr. Rockware Glass
Ltd: front cover cl, back cover, 9tr, 11b, 12t, 12b, 13t, 14t, 14b, 15t, 20, 21t, 24, 25t, 26bl, 27c,
27tr. Heini Schneebeli/SPL: 17t, 26br. Science & Society Picture Library: 21b.
Sygma/Corbis: 23bl. Watts: 3, 28-29, 30br. Whitestone Diomedia/Alamy: 31lc. Daniel E.
Wray/Image Works/Topfoto: 30tr. Every attempt has been made to clear copyright.
Should there be any inadvertent omission please apply to the publisher for rectification.

With thanks to Pilkington plc and Rockware Glass Ltd.
See www.rockware.co.uk for an animated drawing of how
glass bottles and jars are made.

A CIP catalogue record for this book is available from the
British Library.

Printed in Malaysia

Contents

4   This jar is made from glass.

6   Glass is made from sand, limestone and soda ash.

8   The materials arrive at the glass factory.

10   Our jar is mostly made from recycled glass.

12   People and machines clean the glass.

14   The recycled glass is crushed.

16   The materials are placed in a furnace and heated.

18   A machine fires the gobs of glass into jar-shaped moulds.

20   The hot jars leave the forming machine.

22   Every single jar is checked to make sure it is perfect.

24   The jar is ready to leave the factory.

26   How a recycled glass jar is made

28   Amazing glass

32   Word bank

32   Index

This jar is made from glass.

▲ This glass jar is made from clear glass.

The glass in this jar began as heaps of sand, limestone and soda ash. It also has some recycled glass added to it. These materials turn into glass when they are mixed together and heated to a high temperature.

Glass is hard to define. Some people call it a liquid. When glass is hot it moves around like water but as it cools it becomes stiffer, but in fact remains a liquid. However, others call it a solid because when it is cool it keeps its shape.

Before the glass factory begins to make the jar, the workers talk to the customer - the company which needs jars for its food product. They discuss what will be put in the jar and its shape, size and colour. A designer creates pictures of various jar shapes. The customer can choose the one they want.

▲ Designers use computers to show the customer what the jar might look like.

Now the factory starts to make the jar, and many more like it.

Why use glass?

Glass is a good material to use for food and drink storage because it can be cleaned easily and it does not rot. It can be used to store almost everything. Glass is see-through so people can see what is inside the jar and how much is left. People have been using glass containers for thousands of years.

Glass jars help to keep wet and dry foods fresh.

Glass is made from sand, limestone and soda ash.

Sand is the most important raw material for making glass. It is made up of rock and shells that have been broken down over time into tiny grains by the weather and water. People use machines to dig sand out of huge pits in the ground, called quarries.

A digger at work in a sand quarry.

Limestone is another material used to make glass. It formed in the earth millions of years ago from dead sea creatures. Again, people use machines to dig limestone from quarries. The limestone and sand are taken to the glass factory by lorry, boat or train.

A limestone quarry leaves a huge hole in the ground.

A smaller amount of another material, called soda ash, is needed to make glass. Most soda ash is made in factories from salt and other chemicals. Some soda ash can be found naturally in dried-up lakes.

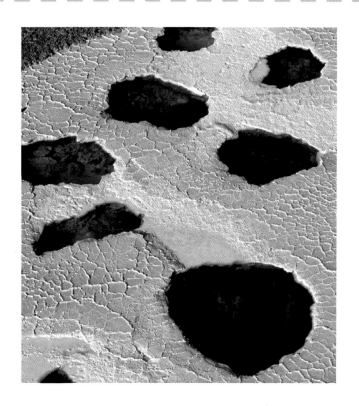

➤ Natron, a kind of soda ash, forms as a crust on some lakes.

Who made the first glass?

Most historians believe that the people living where Syria is today, made the first glass about 5,000 years ago. It is not clear how they discovered glass-making, but perhaps it was an accident. Maybe someone lit a fire on a sandy shore where limestone and soda ash happened to be present in the sand. Tiny drops of glass may have formed at the edge of the fire.

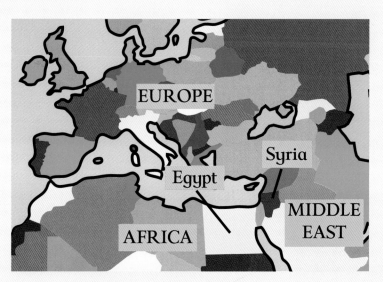

This map shows the area where glass-making began - in modern-day Syria.

The materials arrive at the glass factory.

Sand

Soda ash

Limestone

◄ The ingredients we use to make glass.

The glass-workers unload the raw materials and take them into the batch house. Here the workers carefully weigh out the correct amounts of sand, limestone and soda ash that are needed to make the glass.

Now the raw materials are moved into the furnace. This is a very hot place that looks like a huge baker's oven. It works all day, all year long. Here the raw materials melt together to form molten glass.

Sand on its own can be made into glass, but it has to be heated to an incredibly high temperature - about 1,700°C. By adding limestone and soda ash to the sand, the materials form glass at a much lower temperature.

▲ The furnace heats up the sand, limestone and soda ash to around 700°C and molten glass forms. This is very hot - for example, water boils at 100°C.

In the past

Historians believe the first glass bottles were made by the ancient Egyptians 3,500 years ago. They made bottles by forming a bottle shape from sand and dung, and then dipping it in molten glass several times. When the bottle was cool, it was possible to shake the sand mould out of the inside of the bottle. The bottles were used for perfume, make-up and precious oils and medicines.

A perfume or medicine bottle made by the ancient Egyptians. It was decorated by adding strands of hot, coloured glass to the newly-formed bottle.

Our jar is mostly made from recycled glass.

Recycled glass is made from used glass jars and bottles. People put their used glass into bottle banks or outside their homes for collection. The glass is taken with the rest of their recycling, such as paper and plastic.

▲ In certain areas it is important to keep the recycling in separate containers.

Special recycling lorries collect used glass from people's homes, or the bottle banks, each week or fortnight.

◀ A worker tips the recycling into a collection lorry.

All the used glass arrives at the glass-recycling factory. The lorry empties its load of glass, which is then crushed.

➤ All glass containers can be recycled, not just jars.

A moving belt, called a conveyor belt, takes some broken glass up into the factory.

▲ This used green glass begins its journey to be recycled.

In the past

People used to return empty glass bottles back to where they had bought them. The shopkeeper would pay them a small amount of money in exchange for each empty bottle. Then the bottles were taken back to the original food or drink factory, cleaned, refilled and sold back to the shops. This still happens in some countries. It means that the bottles can be used over and over again.

People and machines clean the glass.

Any materials that are mixed in with the glass need to be removed. The broken glass is moved through the factory on conveyor belts. First it passes under magnets. This removes any iron or steel bits.

▲ The glass passes under strong magnets inside the white triangle-shaped pieces. Any magnetic metal sticks to the magnets.

Then another machine detects and removes any broken bits of ceramics, such as broken cups or plates. Ceramics will damage the furnace.

◀ This machine has lasers inside that detect ceramics.

Workers pick out any objects or pieces that are not glass, as the broken glass passes in front of them.

◀ The workers wear thick gloves to stop themselves from being cut by the glass.

Why use glass?

Glass is an attractive material to work with. Even everyday glass bottles sparkle when they are clean. This has led artists and craftspeople to use glass to make beautiful pictures and designs. By adding different chemicals to the glass mixture, you can create a huge range of different coloured glass. This 'stained glass' has been used in many buildings.

Beautiful patterns and pictures can be created with stained glass.

The recycled glass is crushed.

A crusher smashes the already broken recycled glass into smaller pieces. This finely crushed glass is called cullet. A conveyor belt takes the cullet out of the factory. It is kept in huge mountains until it is needed.

◄ Conveyor belts move the glass around the factory.

▼ Heaps of cullet await use.

Our jar is made from clear glass so it needs some new sand, limestone and soda ash, as well as clear glass cullet. These materials arrive at the factory by lorry, just as they would to make brand new glass (see pages 8-9). Workers weigh the correct amounts of each material and it is taken to the furnace room.

Why use recycled glass?

There are three main reasons to do this:

1. It takes lots of energy to make glass from just sand, limestone and soda ash. Recycled glass does not have to be heated to such a high temperature. This creates less pollution.

2. The more we use recycled glass, the less we have to dig up the landscape for new raw materials. This process uses up energy and destroys the countryside.

3. Using recycled glass encourages people to keep glass separate from the rest of their waste. Unfortunately, large amounts of glass still end up in landfill sites, where the glass is lost for ever. Landfill sites take up lots of space, and it is not pleasant to live near one. Landfills are costly to run.

The materials are placed in a furnace and heated.

The furnace melts the materials and changes them into molten glass. This is very hot glass that is runny like treacle or honey. Rivers of glass leave the furnace to go to the part of the factory where they will be turned into jars.

▽ When the glass leaves the furnace it is very hot.

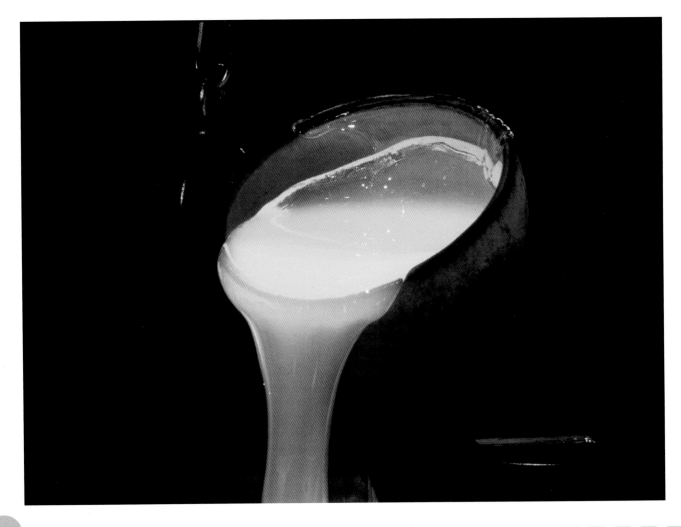

As the molten glass cools, a machine with huge scissors cuts it into equal-sized pieces, called gobs. The factory workers have set the machine to make the gobs just the right size for a glass jar.

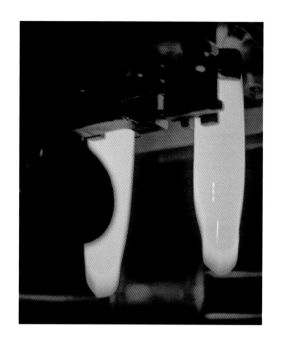

➤ Gobs of hot glass pass along to the next machine.

Why use glass?

Once it is in a molten state, glass can be made into a wide range of shapes and sizes. One of the greatest uses for glass is as flat panes of glass for windows. Panes of glass are called float glass because they are made by floating hot, molten glass on a bath of molten metal, usually tin. The glass spreads out and gradually hardens as it cools. It passes over cooling rollers until it is hard enough to be cut into the correct size for windows.

The raw materials are fed into the float glass furnace.

The materials melt in the furnace.

A machine fires the gobs of glass into jar-shaped moulds.

These moulds are part of the forming machine. A piece of the machine seals the top of the mould once the glass gob is inside. Then, from the bottom, a plunger moves up inside the gob, pushing the glass out to the mould's sides.

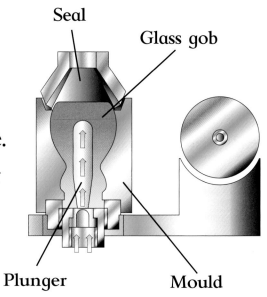

Seal

Glass gob

Plunger

Mould

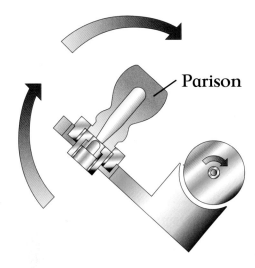

Parison

The mould opens to reveal the partly-shaped jar, upside down and still very hot. At this point the jar is called a parison. The forming machine now turns the parison the other way up, onto its base.

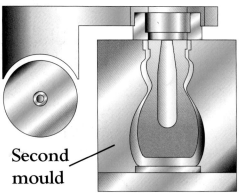

Second mould

A second, slightly bigger, mould closes around it.

The glass slowly runs down, until it reaches the bottom of this second mould.

The machine now blows jets of air into the jar, pushing the hot glass out to the sides of the mould. Now the glass is thinner and the jar is bigger.

Jets of air

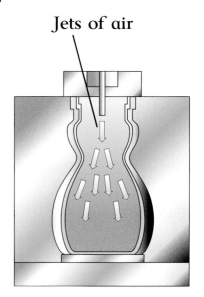

In the past

Glass-blowing is a way of making glass containers by blowing air inside molten glass. People learned how to do this in the first century BCE. The glass-blower dipped his hollow pipe into molten glass and then slowly turned the pipe round and round. He then rolled the glass gob on an iron slab, blew air down the pipe to expand the gob, and reheated the glass back in the fire so that he could keep working with it. Eventually, the glass-blower finished the object and cut it off his pipe. He then allowed it to cool down.

In this 19th-century drawing, French glass-blowers are making bottles by blowing air down long pipes.

The hot jars leave the forming machine.

▲ Tongs pick up the hot jars and take them off the forming machine.

Cold air blows around the jar to cool it off. The jar is placed on a conveyor belt and travels away from the forming machine to a large oven called a lehr. On the way to the lehr, the surface of each jar is given a coating to make it stronger during its lifetime.

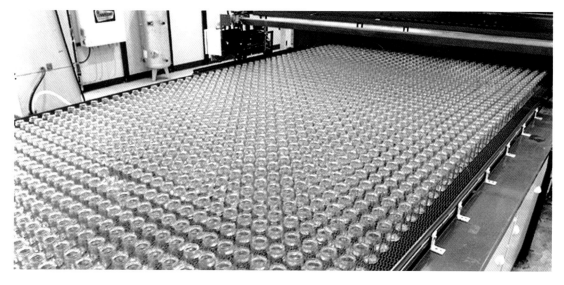

◀ The jars leave the lehr after 20 to 40 minutes.

In the lehr, the jar heats up to 550°C and then cools down gradually. This removes any cracks or weak points that may have been created during the forming process. As the jar leaves the lehr, the outside is coated again to stop it forming scratches easily.

In the past

For almost 2,000 years, glass jars and bottles were made by glass-blowing. Then, in 1886, Howard Ashley, from the UK, finished the design of a machine able to make 200 glass bottles an hour. Unfortunately, he didn't manage to make his invention successful. Then, in 1903, Michael J Owens, from Illinois, USA, developed a much faster, fully automatic, bottle-making machine making 2,500 glass bottles per hour. His machines were used for decades.

A glass bust of Michael J Owens made by the Owens Bottle Company.

Every single jar is checked to make sure it is perfect.

The jar passes through machinery that automatically checks for problems. The machines can check whether the glass in the jar is the correct thickness and can spot any cracks or other problems. Any jars that aren't good enough to be used end up back in the recycled glass mountains to be melted down.

▼ The rejected glass piles up ready to be recycled.

If the machines do find problems,
then this information will be sent
back to the beginning of the process,
so that the machinery can be altered.

Why use glass?

Glass can be shaped in many ways. Some bottles and jars have such a special shape that we know instantly what will be inside them. The Coca-Cola company started selling their famous drink in shaped glass bottles in 1915. Heinz Tomato Ketchup is another bottle shape that many people recognise. Marmite has been sold in brown jars that have hardly changed shape in 100 years.

Do you know what is inside these bottles?

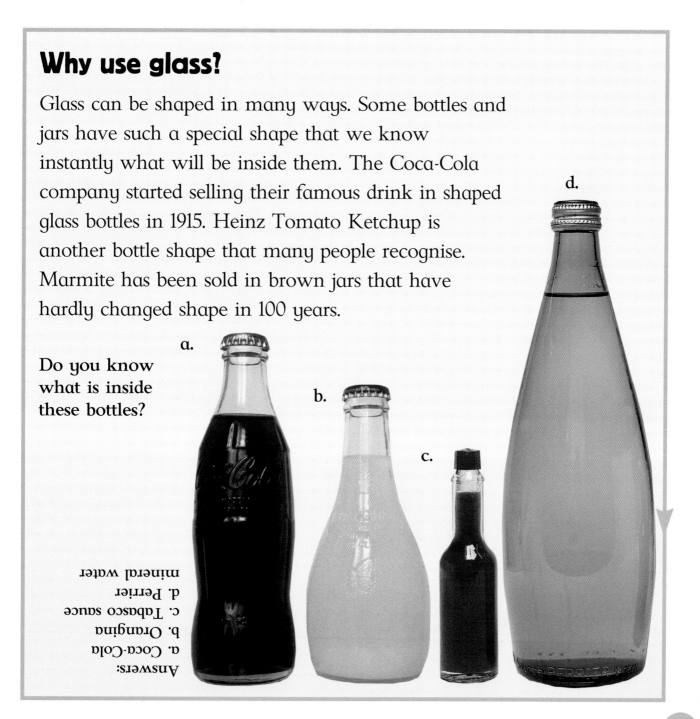

Answers:
a. Coca-Cola
b. Orangina
c. Tabasco sauce
d. Perrier mineral water

The jar is ready to leave the factory.

As more and more jars are finished, they are packed into trays. Workers stack up the trays into towers. To stop the jars from moving about and knocking against each other, machines wrap the trays tightly in plastic.

Now all that needs to happen is for the jars to travel to the food factory that asked for them to be made. At this factory, machines fill the jars with food such as fruit, coffee, jam or olives. A plastic screw lid is added to finish.

◄ These jars are being filled with coffee.

Another machine sticks a label on the jar and it is finally ready to be sold in the shops.

When the jar is empty it can be recycled. Then the glass in the jar is made into a new jar - maybe in a different shape - at the glass recycling factory.

► The label tells us what is in the jar.

John Landis Mason with his Mason jars.

In the past

Hundreds of people designed glass jars for preserving fruit and vegetables, but John Landis Mason's are the most famous. In 1858 he invented a metal screw lid, which screwed onto his jars to seal the contents quickly and effectively. People continue to use Mason jars in the USA today. The original ones are worth a lot of money.

How a recycled glass jar is made

1. Sand, limestone and soda ash arrive at the glass-recycling factory.

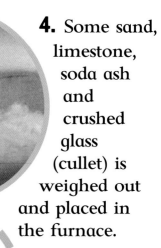

4. Some sand, limestone, soda ash and crushed glass (cullet) is weighed out and placed in the furnace.

2. Used glass bottles and jars arrive at the glass-recycling factory.

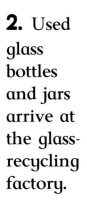

5. Glass forms in the furnace and leaves as rivers of molten glass.

3. The recycled glass is cleaned to remove any unwanted material.

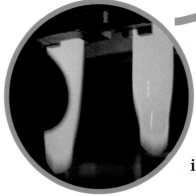

6. The molten glass is cut into gobs.

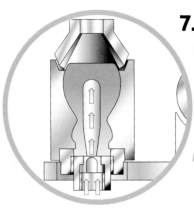

7. The forming machine makes the glass jar.

10. The jar is filled with food and sent off to shops to be sold.

8. The glass jar travels into the lehr, where it is heated up and then slowly cools down.

11. The full jar.

9. The jar is checked for cracks or problems. Some jars are rejected and recycled.

Amazing glass

Look around you to see how many different types of glass you can see.

➤ Have you ever used a telescope or a microscope? Glass lenses are used in these instruments to bring distant objects closer or make small objects bigger.

Is anyone wearing glasses? Special glass can be shaped to make lenses for glasses so that people can see clearly.

◁ Is the light on? The outside of an electric light bulb is made from glass.

Is there a television or computer in the room? Most screens are made from a special sort of glass that contains lead or barium. The lead and barium absorb harmful X-rays that would otherwise escape from the TV or computer.

Are there any beautiful glass ornaments or glass objects in the room? By adding lead to glass, it makes it sparkle and shine. It also makes it easier to cut and engrave to add to its beauty.

Do you need a drink? Glass is made into containers that we can drink from.

➤ If you are in the kitchen, you may see special types of strong glass that are used for parts of the cooker, and to make pots and pans that can be heated without breaking.

➤ In the bathroom, the mirror is made from glass, coated on the back with a thin layer of silver, or another shiny metal, to make it reflect your face.

▲ Up in the loft of your home or school, matted strands of glass, called glass wool, help to trap heat like a blanket.

➤ Is there anyone outside? We look through panes of glass in our windows and doors.

◀When mixed with plastic, glass fibres make a material called Fibreglass. It can be mixed with other materials to make helmets, parts of cars and boats like the body of this speed boat.

➤ Glass can be made shatterproof by adding a layer of thin material like plastic. Then this strengthened glass is used to make the windscreens of cars, rockets and tanks. Whole buildings can be covered with glass.

Word bank

Conveyor belt A moving belt or band used to transport goods or objects around a factory.

Cullet The name given to finely broken glass.

Forming machine The machine that changes the hot gobs of glass into glass jars or bottles, using moulds.

Landfill site A huge hole in the ground used for burying waste.

Lehr A huge oven, or kiln, used to heat the glass jars.

Molten A material which is so hot that it has melted into a runny liquid.

Mould A container that gives shape to glass and other materials.

Parison A partly-shaped lump of glass that will become a jar or bottle.

Raw material A material that is still in its natural state. The raw materials used to make glass are sand, limestone and soda ash.

Recycling The process of collecting and reusing many everyday objects, from newspapers to glass jars.

Index

bank, bottle 10

chemical 7, 13
cullet 14, 26, 32

factory, glass 5, 6, 8
   glass-recycling 11-14, 16, 25, 26
   forming machine 18-20, 27, 32
   furnace 8, 9, 12, 14, 16, 17, 26

glass,
   cleaning 12-13, 26
   crushing 11, 14, 26, 32
   glass-blowing 19, 21

glass (continued)
   gob 17, 18, 19, 32
   history of 7, 9, 19, 21, 25
   ingredients of 6-9
   molten 8, 9, 16, 17, 19, 26, 32
   recycled 4, 10-15, 22, 25, 26, 32
   stained 13
   types of 28-31
   window 17

jar,
   checking 22-23, 27
   designing 5
   filling 24, 27

jar (continued)
   moulding 18-19, 26, 32
   strengthening 20-21

lehr 20-21, 27, 32
limestone 4, 6-9, 14, 15, 26, 32

materials, raw 6-7, 8, 15, 17, 32

parison 18, 19, 32

sand 4, 6-9, 14, 15, 26, 32
soda ash 4, 6-9, 14, 15, 26, 32